WALKING THE CAMINO

SUPPLEMENTARY WORKBOOK

Julia Goodfellow-Smith

Walking the Camino: Supplementary Workbook
Published by Julia Goodfellow-Smith

First published in 2023
Copyright © Julia Goodfellow-Smith

The right of Julia Goodfellow-Smith to be identified as the author of this work has been asserted by her in accordance with the Copyright, Designs and Patent Act 1988.

All rights reserved. No part of this publication may be reproduced, stored in or introduced into a retrieval system, distributed or transmitted in any form or by any means, including photocopying, recording, or other electronic or mechanical methods, without the prior written permission of the publisher, except in the case of brief quotations embodied in critical reviews and certain other non-commercial uses permitted by copyright law.

This book is sold subject to the condition that it shall not, by way of trade or otherwise, be lent, re-sold, hired out, or otherwise circulated without the publisher's prior consent in any form of binding or cover other than that in which it is published and without a similar condition including this condition being imposed on the subsequent purchaser.

Although the author and publisher have made every effort to ensure that the information in this book was correct at press time, the author and publisher do not assume and hereby disclaim any liability to any party for any loss, damage, or disruption caused by errors or omissions, whether such errors or omissions result from negligence, accident, or any other cause.

Neither the author nor the publisher assumes any responsibility or liability whatsoever on behalf of the consumer or reader of this material. Any perceived slight of any individual or organization is purely unintentional.

ISBN: 978-0-86319-491-7

Table of Contents

Introduction	1
Ignite Your Dream	**3**
Define Your Dream	5
Smash Your Stumbling Blocks	14
Make a Decision - and Mean It	18
Make a Plan	**27**
Break Down Your Journey into Stages	29
Do Not Reinvent the Wheel	41
Hope for the Best and Plan for the Worst	52
Use Your Superpowers and Sidestep Your Achilles Heels	64
Find the Time You Need	69
Find the Money You Need	72

Implement Your Plan	**75**
Give Yourself an Assisted Boost	77
Look After Yourself	79
Ride the Storm	83
Reflect	**87**
Reaching Santiago – Celebrate and Reflect	89
An Invitation	97
Books by Julia Goodfellow-Smith	99
About the Author	101

Introduction

Walking the Camino is an extraordinary experience, as illustrated in my book **Walking the Camino**. Use this workbook to answer the questions raised in **Walking the Camino** and plan your own pilgrimage. The four-part structure of igniting your dream, planning, implementing your plan and reflecting is detailed in another of my books, **Live Your Bucket List: Simple Steps to Ignite Your Dreams, Face Your Fears and Lead an Extraordinary Life, Starting Today.**

Check out www.juliags.com/caminolinks for links to useful resources.

Ignite Your Dream

Define Your Dream

How far do you want to walk?
Or for how long?

_____

_____

_____

_____

_____

_____

_____

_____

_____

_____

_____

_____

_____

How far do you want to walk each day?

Will you take rest days?

_____
_____
_____
_____
_____
_____
_____
_____
_____
_____
_____
_____
_____
_____
_____
_____
_____
_____

What time of year do you want to walk?

Which Camino route do you want to take?

See Appendix 1 of **Walking the Camino** for some suggestions about how to choose.

_____
_____
_____
_____
_____
_____
_____
_____
_____
_____
_____
_____
_____
_____
_____
_____

Will you carry your luggage or use a transfer service?

What type of accommodation would you prefer?

See Appendix 2 of **Walking the Camino** for information about the choices available.

_____
_____
_____
_____
_____
_____
_____
_____
_____
_____
_____
_____
_____
_____
_____
_____
_____
_____

Are you going to walk alone, with a friend or in a group?

Will you organise everything yourself or join an organised tour?

Smash Your Stumbling Blocks

What are your reasons for not having walked the Camino already?

These might include a lack of fitness, not having someone to walk with, needing to save up, or struggling to find the time.

_____
_____
_____
_____
_____
_____
_____
_____
_____
_____
_____
_____
_____

Are there any other reasons you can think of why you might shy away from the challenge now?

_____
_____
_____
_____
_____
_____
_____
_____
_____
_____
_____
_____
_____
_____
_____
_____
_____

What limiting beliefs do you have that might stop you, e.g. I'm too old, too young, not good enough, can't afford it? What do you fear if you pursue this dream?

_____
_____
_____
_____
_____
_____
_____
_____
_____
_____
_____
_____
_____
_____

For each of these potential stumbling blocks, what can you do to smash or sidestep it?

_____
_____
_____
_____
_____
_____
_____
_____
_____
_____
_____
_____
_____
_____
_____
_____
_____
_____
_____
_____

Make a Decision – and Mean It

Why do you want to walk the Camino?

List all your reasons on the left.

Why do you NOT want to walk the Camino?

List all your reasons on the right.

Now, draw arrows towards the centre line that reflect the strength of that reason.

Do the positives outweigh the negatives? If not, is there anything you can do to strengthen the positives or reduce the significance of the negatives?

_____
_____
_____
_____
_____
_____
_____
_____
_____
_____
_____
_____
_____
_____
_____
_____

Picture yourself standing outside Santiago cathedral. How will you feel once you have achieved your dream?

_____
_____
_____
_____
_____
_____
_____
_____
_____
_____
_____
_____
_____
_____
_____
_____

Who or what will you be grateful for?

_____
_____
_____
_____
_____
_____
_____
_____
_____
_____
_____
_____
_____
_____
_____
_____
_____

What skills have you developed?

What challenges will you have overcome?

How will you feel if you don't pursue your Camino dream? Imagine how you will feel in a year, five years and ten years.

_____
_____
_____
_____
_____
_____
_____
_____
_____
_____
_____
_____
_____
_____
_____
_____
_____
_____

How does this compare to being committed to achieving your goal?

Make a Plan

Make a Plan

Break Down Your Journey into Stages

What needs to be on your kit list?

Check out my packing list in Appendix 4 of **Walking the Camino.**

_____

_____

_____

_____

_____

_____

_____

_____

_____

_____

_____

_____

What do you need to acquire?

Make a Plan

Do you have a comfortable backpack that's the right size?

_____

_____

_____

_____

_____

_____

_____

_____

_____

_____

_____

_____

_____

_____

_____

_____

_____

What will you wear on your feet?
Do you need to wear in your shoes or boots?

Make a Plan

What training do you need to do? How long do you think you will need to get fit enough?

_____

_____

_____

_____

_____

_____

_____

_____

_____

_____

_____

_____

_____

_____

_____

_____

How are you going to get to the starting point?

___

Make a Plan

Do you want to book accommodation for the first couple of days?

_____

_____

_____

_____

_____

_____

_____

_____

_____

_____

_____

_____

_____

_____

_____

_____

_____

Do you need to book time off work or other commitments?

Make a Plan

How can you make time to reflect and recover on your return?

_____

_____

_____

_____

_____

_____

_____

_____

_____

_____

_____

_____

_____

_____

_____

_____

_____

If you want to turn your Camino into a pilgrimage rather than just a long-distance walk, how will you do that?

_____
_____
_____
_____
_____
_____
_____
_____
_____
_____
_____
_____
_____
_____
_____

Make a Plan

Do you have questions you would like to ponder? If so, what are they?

See Appendix 5 of **Walking the Camino** for some suggested prompts.

_____
_____
_____
_____
_____
_____
_____
_____
_____
_____
_____
_____
_____
_____
_____
_____

Are there people you want to think about and light candles for? If so, who – and why?

Make a Plan

Do Not Reinvent the Wheel

Who do you know who could help you prepare for the Camino, either spiritually or practically?

_____
_____
_____
_____
_____
_____
_____
_____
_____
_____
_____
_____

What books could you read?

Make a Plan

What YouTube videos could you watch?

Which podcasts could you listen to?

Make a Plan

What Facebook groups or other forums could you join?

_____
_____
_____
_____
_____
_____
_____
_____
_____
_____
_____
_____
_____
_____
_____
_____

Do you have a backup map, e.g. on the Buen Camino app?

___
___
___
___
___
___
___
___
___
___
___
___
___
___
___
___

Have you weighed your pack? Could you make it any lighter by switching kit for lighter versions or leaving something out?

Have you bought your pilgrim passport (a 'credencial')?

Make a Plan

Have you considered learning some Spanish?

Do you want to take any dietary supplements with you?

Make a Plan

If you are walking the Francés route, will you carry a stone representing a burden you would like to leave behind at the Iron Cross? If so, what is that burden?

_____
_____
_____
_____
_____
_____
_____
_____
_____
_____
_____
_____
_____
_____

Hope for the Best and Plan for the Worst

What's your preferred method of dealing with blisters? Do you have a blister treatment kit on your kit list?

_____
_____
_____
_____
_____
_____
_____
_____
_____
_____
_____
_____
_____

Make a Plan

Do you have any physical weaknesses or injuries you need to consider, e.g. a knee that might need strapping?

_____
_____
_____
_____
_____
_____
_____
_____
_____
_____
_____
_____
_____
_____
_____
_____
_____

Do you know basic first aid?

Make a Plan

What do you need in your first aid kit?

Do you know the signs of dehydration or heat stroke? What can you do to avoid these conditions?

Make a Plan

Do you have travel insurance?

If you're from the UK, do you have a Global Health Insurance Card?

Make a Plan

What would you do if someone stole your pack or other valuables?

How will you protect yourself from any unfriendly dogs you encounter?

Make a Plan

Are you taking any essential medication? Is it on your packing list?

_____

_____

_____

_____

_____

_____

_____

_____

_____

_____

_____

_____

_____

_____

_____

_____

_____

What will you do if you need to pee or poo and are nowhere near a toilet?

_____
_____
_____
_____
_____
_____
_____
_____
_____
_____
_____
_____
_____
_____
_____
_____
_____

Make a Plan

What other contingency situations do you foresee?

_____

_____

_____

_____

_____

_____

_____

_____

_____

_____

_____

_____

_____

_____

_____

_____

_____

Use Your Superpowers and Sidestep Your Achilles Heels

What superpowers do you have?

_____
_____
_____
_____
_____
_____
_____
_____
_____
_____
_____
_____
_____
_____

Make a Plan

How can you use these to help you achieve your Camino dream?

_____

_____

_____

_____

_____

_____

_____

_____

_____

_____

_____

_____

_____

_____

_____

_____

How can you use these to support others while on the Camino?

Make a Plan

What weaknesses do you have?

How can you sidestep, manage or overcome them?

Find the Time You Need

When can you fit in training?
Is there something else that you need to stop doing for a while to give yourself more time?

_____
_____
_____
_____
_____
_____
_____
_____
_____
_____
_____
_____
_____
_____
_____

Do you need to book time off work for the trip itself? If you can't take enough time off to walk the entire route, could you walk it in sections instead?

_____
_____
_____
_____
_____
_____
_____
_____
_____
_____
_____
_____
_____
_____
_____

Make a Plan

How will you carve out some time to reflect on your experience on your return?

_____
_____
_____
_____
_____
_____
_____
_____
_____
_____
_____
_____
_____
_____
_____
_____
_____

Find the Money You Need

How much money do you need for your trip?

Estimate the cost of each part of your trip and create a budget below. Remember to include travel costs, direct costs while walking, indirect costs, equipment, insurance, visas and contingencies.

Make a Plan

If you need to reduce cost, how will you do that?

How long will you need to save up, or can you pay for it from your savings or income?

Implement Your Plan

Give Yourself an Assisted Boost

What mantras could you adopt to help you when things get tough?

What negative stories do you tell yourself that might get in the way?
What can you do to change these stories?

_____
_____
_____
_____
_____
_____
_____
_____
_____
_____
_____
_____
_____
_____
_____
_____
_____

Look After Yourself

How will you look after your health while training and walking the route?

Do you need to ask someone to be more positive or supportive?

Implement Your Plan

Do you need to avoid someone while you are completing this challenge to protect your positive state of mind?

_____
_____
_____
_____
_____
_____
_____
_____
_____
_____
_____
_____
_____
_____
_____
_____

If you are an introvert, how will you ensure you have enough time to recharge between social interactions?

_____
_____
_____
_____
_____
_____
_____
_____
_____
_____
_____
_____
_____
_____
_____
_____
_____

Ride the Storm

Sometimes, an unforeseen event will threaten to knock you off course. If that happens, try reviewing your reason for walking the Camino. Then consider your options:

Do you need to shift your attention to deal with this unforeseen event and park your pilgrimage dream for now?

_____

_____

_____

_____

_____

_____

_____

_____

_____

_____

Can you adapt your plans, e.g. tackling a shorter route closer to home?

_____
_____
_____
_____
_____
_____
_____
_____
_____
_____
_____
_____
_____
_____
_____

Implement Your Plan

Are there any new advantages to gain from this unforeseen event?

Can you still do something towards your Camino dream? If not, is it time to consider tackling another bucket list dream while you can't pursue this one?

_____
_____
_____
_____
_____
_____
_____
_____
_____
_____
_____
_____
_____
_____
_____

Reflect

Reaching Santiago - Celebrate and Reflect

How do you feel now you've finished your pilgrimage?

_____
_____
_____
_____
_____
_____
_____
_____
_____
_____
_____
_____
_____

How are you going to mark your achievement?

Reflect

How will you consolidate your memories?

___

What have you learnt about yourself on the Camino?

_____
_____
_____
_____
_____
_____
_____
_____
_____
_____
_____
_____
_____
_____
_____

Reflect

What have you learnt about others?

_____
_____
_____
_____
_____
_____
_____
_____
_____
_____
_____
_____
_____
_____
_____
_____
_____
_____
_____

How have you changed, or how would you like to change?

Reflect

How will you apply this learning to your everyday life?

_____

_____

_____

_____

_____

_____

_____

_____

_____

_____

_____

_____

_____

_____

_____

_____

An Invitation

Congratulations on reaching the end of your Camino journey! If you have found this workbook useful, then you will love **Live Your Bucket List**, which guides you through this process in more detail. It will support you through your journey to achieve any of your bucket list dreams, from deciding which to pursue first; igniting your passion for that dream; overcoming obstacles such as fear, lack of money and time; planning to achieve your dream; implementing your plans; and reflecting on your journey. You can pick it up wherever you usually buy books from or listen to the audiobook on all the normal channels.

You can listen to the introduction and first three chapters of **Live Your Bucket List**, free of charge, at www.juliags.com/members.

I always appreciate receiving feedback so I can make the next version of this and future books better. I love hearing what you have to say — please leave me an honest review or email me.

And if you are looking for an inspiring and entertaining speaker for a meeting, event or broadcast, please give me a shout.

julia@juliags.com
www.juliags.com
 @juliagsauthor
 @juliagsauthorspeaker
 @juliagsauthorspeaker

Books by Julia Goodfellow-Smith

Live Your Bucket List series
- Live Your Bucket List: Simple Steps to Ignite Your Dreams, Face Your Fears and Lead an Extraordinary Life, Starting Today
- Cycling King Alfred's Way: A Piece of Cake?
- Walking the Camino: A Journey For the Heart and Soul

Walking guidebooks
- 15 Short Walks on the Malvern Hills, Cicerone Press
- Top 10 Coastal Pub Walks: South Wales, Northern Eye Books

www.juliags.com/writing

About the Author

Julia Goodfellow-Smith is an ordinary person who is doing something extraordinary — living her bucket list. In recent years, she has discovered a love of hiking, which is why she leapt at the chance of walking the Camino.

Julia has held a variety of management and consultancy roles in a range of sectors including conservation volunteering, banking and construction. She is currently focusing her attention on adventure, writing and presenting.

Julia lives in Wales with her husband Mike, and loves their daily walks along the beach. She is a member of Rotary International, a Fellow of the Royal Society of Arts and a Senator of Junior Chamber International (JCI).

www.ingramcontent.com/pod-product-compliance
Lightning Source LLC
Chambersburg PA
CBHW032045290426
44110CB00012B/963